the

VOICE

OF

EXPERIENCE

By Kenechi C. Anene

PREFACE

This motivational book is a composition of real life experiences of a boy turned man within a space of six years.

95% of the writings were experienced real life and written down in a concise summarized manner for straight to point understanding, while the rest are gotten from secondary data collection which include, discussions, radio, television, books, etc.

The book contains some characters that were experienced during the harsh and bitter times hence the harsh conclusion which may not be aptly described as the proper conclusion but was written down as well. Most of these biased conclusions were indicated with the questions mark in parenthesis (?).

Some of the quotations as already explained were gotten from secondary data collection and the means were not quoted except for Gandhi and few others. The original quotes should please forgive my incompetence because most of them were gotten during the heat of moments and these quotes aptly describes the moment, so I took them without further research.

As you read, try to assimilate at least 50% of the information into your life and notice the changed person you will become, remember it's the '*Voice of Experience*'.

Thanks.
KC Anene.

ACKNOWLEDGMENT

I immensely thank those who knowingly or unknowingly assisted in the creation of this my journal.

Also those that pushed me unknowingly into publishing it, my publisher inclusive. Ngozi Eluma who unknowingly inspired me into doing this, Ifeanyi Oliver, who kept taunting me throughout the period I was processing it, Precious Okorie, who promised to assist me but never got herself to do it, my parents, Mr. & Mrs. John. Obinwa Anene who gave me a breathing space, etc.

May the one you believe in guide you in all your endeavors.

KC Anene.

DEDICATION

In memory of
Okezie Chukwudinma (Augustus) Anene,
The one true brother I ever had.
May his soul Rest in Peace.

DATE	EXPERIENCE
27/12/04	Friends are unreliable, don't over trust them
"	Weather changes my mood, dull weather = moody me. Is it psychological or what?
"	What you think is what you are
"	Postponing the problem isn't the solution. Solve it first
28 / "	Sometimes disappointment comes from your best bet
"	Why is it that when you need day, night comes?
29 / "	Life is better observed when you are a spectator
"	Life is best observed when you are a participator
"	When the enemy shows a different character, it doesn't necessarily mean repentance. It might be a strategy.
"	Love doesn't fade easily, so is emotion
31 / "	To forget your past is easier said that done.
"	You opponent is always looking for ways to surpass you, don't be over-relaxed

GOODBYE 20-04 WELCOME 20-05

01/01/05   It started bad; think the worst is over because I see the sun smiling at me right now.

"   Blaming the past for the present condition is unfair because the present doesn't know the future.

"   Why is it that those you didn't wish evil do it to you?

"   Happy expectation makes a happy soul.

02 / "   Always be ready for disappointments, so that the blow wouldn't be harsh when it falls.

"   Looks can be deceptive.

03 / "   Why do lies taste so sweet in the mouth?

"   When you feel like hope is gone, keep your head up cause behind you comes the light, if you believe.

"   Loneliness is very dangerous, escape from it as quick as you can.

"   God don't respect the prayer, just the faith

"   A man does not climb a thorny tree out of bravado, but because of a goal to achieve

"   Sometimes it's better to forget the present and wait for the future

"   It's only kids that seek attention

"   Most times we displease God to please fellow human

"   There's no man without problem, it's just that the problem varies.

13 / "   When you concentrate on others fault, you wouldn't be able to see yours

"   Forgive me my trespasses, as I forgive those that trespasses against me

14 / "   When you are enjoying life, remember that they are others that are doing the exact opposite

01/03/05   When the lost one is gone, you don't feel any emotion

"   When progress is prolonged, it becomes frustration

02 / "   On the way to success, some toes would be trodden on.

03 / "   Don't expect your friends to welcome you with open arms @ all time.

"   They are friends but there is a true friend

16 / "   For you to forgive easily, see those that wronged you as your teacher in experience.

"   You have to love before you are to be loved

"   When a friend betrays you, take it as God's way of saying "he/she isn't your friend"

"   The He said, "Father Forgive Them for they Don't Know What they Are Doing"

"   As I'm emotionally sensitive person, the Devil will love to hurt my emotions.

"   Friend is he who is looking for a reason to come in when others are going out.

"   When you are wronged, look at it from the right angle. (take it as a good experience)

17 / "   Show me a man without problem and I will show you a man that exists in grave

" And she told Him, "Lord see the one you love is sick".

" He said "this sickness is for the Glory of God"

" No cross no crown

" When He Heard Of His friend's sickness, He delayed for two more days before going to him

" You can't go to your destination without passing through your destiny.

18 / " Weakness is like a small hole in a dam, it will eventually lead to its collapse it isn't checked.

23 / " God wont give you what you want but what you need.

24 / " You may not die now, but you must die later.

" Don't say 'I cannot afford this' say 'how can I afford this?'

" A friend is the one that can accommodate your foolery

" IF you choose friends when things are fine, you might choose an enemy

" A real friend aims at multiplying your joy and eradicating your grieves.

" Making friends isn't difficult, the maintenance is.

" Friend is like a pillar, he either carry you, stand on you or stand by you.

22 / " Hatred is caused by fear

" Patience is holding your inclination to the seven emotions; hate, Adoration, Joy, Anxiety, Anger, Grief (Shogun)

30 / " The silent will is the strongest

" Envy is caused by inferiority complex

" Don't ever 'guess' and conclude, rather prove before

conclusion.

09/05/05	Don't over-trust, even those that claims loving you
"	To the pure, all things are pure and vice versa
"	Let's try to… forget the past, face the present and be ready for the future.
31 / "	Don't criticize publicly what you admire secretly.
"	Friendship is the highest level of relationship.

06/06/05	Argument is for the proud
"	To forgive is to set a prisoner free
"	It's better to be where you are celebrated than where you are tolerated.
"	Sometimes betrayal helps shape destiny.
"	When closing the doors of relationship, leave at least one open.
"	Learn to be appreciative, it helps a lot
"	Don't lend what you can't afford to lose
"	Try not to borrow to give
"	Frequent attendance causes negligence
"	After your best, leave the rest.
08/ "	When the day gets confusing, don't mourn, keep your head up.
"	Adoration is trust plus love
"	Joy is the happy exclamation of the soul
"	Anxiety is trusting what you cant trust
"	Anger is the temporary madness of a sane person
"	Grief is an outward expression of defeat

"   Fear is when you can subdue what you don't desire

"   Love is becoming a slave to someone you are fond of

"   When you feel like hope is gone, look inside you, set the hero free.

"   The best form of defense is attack

25 / "   In every aspect of life, find the humorous side, tap it but don't milk it dry.

"   You are to be blamed if you leave your pre-destined part for another

"   The latest arsenal is pride hurting

04/09/05   Today I found her after 3 years of break,

Today I found out it was infatuation,

Today am set free.

09 / "   Why is that when you increase the distance, they approach and when you shorten it, they run?

"   Even your sister can betray you in the moment of desperation

10 / "   Begging reduces stature

11 / "   Nothing happens for nothing

"   Face your worst fear because it's what you fear that comes to you

"   Doctors don't stop death, they postpone it

"   Its better to be laughed at than to be cried for

25 / "   You cant believe what you don't know

"   Nothing succeeds like success

"   Even elastic have limit

"	If you don't want doubt, don't listen to victims
"	Smartness is good, uprightness is better

02/10/05	Yesterday is a nightmare that keeps flashing
"	I have to find a better memory fast or …
13 / "	Death is the biggest mystery which we must solve at the end
"	It's easier to ask for forgiveness than for permission
14 / "	Failure is the proof that you've tried
"	It seems like a road is opening

21/11/05	The best way to cure my trouble is by constantly getting in touch with it
24/11/05	Over worrying makes you lose your sense of humor
"	Tomorrow is here, face it and complete your trail
"	Time is shortest when life is sweetest
"	What's my origin before entering this planet?
"	Show me a man without emotion and I will show you a log in the jungle
"	Emotion is for the weak?
25 / "	It's the Nigerians that makes up Nigeria
26 / "	Don't think backwards, think forward
27 / "	You can give what you don't have but please don't give what you don't have
"	Does love liberate or imprison you?
"	The gods cannot do for me what they can do by themselves

"   Don't value the word of mouth till it's done

29 / "   Fear is just four letter word which you can easily erase

05/12/05   Anger is what gets us into trouble … pride is what keeps us there.

06 / "   I'm not a wicked soul as they said, but a grieving one.

"   I fear no one but Jehovah, no place but hell.

07 / "   Staying one place does not help in grieving time, get busy.

"   How can one person have all the keys to my emotions?

"   'Disappointments', it still hurts no matter how prepared you are

14 / "   The feeding of a lion always precedes a funeral in the animal kingdom

15 / "   A traveler doesn't have a thorn lodged in his feet for remembrance sake, rather her removes it and continue.

16 / "   Help yourself, don't pity what you can't help.

20 / "   Gawd!!! What a day, ozo-emena

31 / "   Tonight the last battle was fought, think I lost. Don't cry for me…. Every disappointment …

31/12/05   Tonight I will say die.

GOODBYE 20-05 WELCOME 20-06

03/01/06   I believe this will be my last attempt on love. (?)

"   Phew, that was close. Realized I could have fallen for her and have heartbreak.

04 / "   She is going with December and will be gone with January. (True?)

05 / "   She's got the upper hand since I'm like a soldier going to war without plan.

08 / "   Just because it's all you know doesn't mean it's all you will enjoy.

19 / "   Every lion have it's Daniel and sometimes, it's Samson

20 / "   You don't have to go to the moon to know that it's there

"   Why do I always stand apart from my fellow men? Fear or observing?

23 / "   I'm not a negative but benevolent skeptic

28 / "   Those whom the gods want to kill, they first of all make proud

"   Don't take credit for what you are not responsible for

01/02/06   Pat, your SMS really touched this heart of mine but I'm sorry I'll be silent cos am converting it to a stone.

02 / "   Dead sinners in the hand of the angry God. How terrible!!!

"   The boy will be a man

06 / "   To re-live, the mythical phoenix has to burn. I have burned, I'm now refreshed.

"   Can God lie, or is my case hopeless?

07 / 02   To live longer, trust more of your own sex.

14 / "   Train yourself to let go of everything you fear to lose.

"   All who gain power are afraid to lose it.

15 / "   In doing good things, avoid fame, in doing bad, avoid disgrace.

02/03/06   Beware! I do not bark, I bite.

08 / "   He who's on the ground fears no fall.

30/07/06   Love is for poets?

"   Think with your head and not with your emotion.

02 / "   Show me a man that doesn't lobe and I'll show you a man without soul

"   Never confuse your feelings for your duties

09 / "   A prolonged anger results to bitterness

17 / "   Love comes with pain

18 / "   Can love come once, forever?

04/10/06   I know that you've fallen in love with me; I know you really care but the problem is that I don't have any love to reciprocate.

"   I'll at least try and show care and affection in the absence of love.

"   Now I've made the princess to fall to me, am I satisfied?

"   Sometimes in life, you got to drop some of your luggage no matter how important it is to you in order to make the journey easier.

5 / "   We lived for a moment but for long, I've searched for the one

21 / "   My sweet, no matter what you feel, please don't go till I repay you of your entire kindness tome.

"   When a man ceases to grow, then he dies.

"   When a man stops moving forward, he must out of necessity start going backwards.

"   The rung of the ladder was never meant for resting rather to hold the foot long enough to put the next somewhat higher.

"   Obstacles are those frightful things you see when you take your eyes off the goal.

"   The bee that makes the honey doesn't hang around the hive.

"   Vision without a task is just a dream,
    Task without vision is drudgery,
    Vision and task is the hope of the world.

"   He who seeks to attain the incredible must 1st attempt the impossible.

"   The poor man is not a kobo-less but a dreamless man. `

GOODBYE 20-06 WELCOME 20-07

20/03/05   Darkest time of the night is the nearest time to dawn

"   You must pass through the fire, just pray it doesn't burn you

"   Even elastic have limit

01/04/07   The lion may be the mightiest but it's the chameleon that endures

"   The fear of loss is a pathway to the dark side sometimes.

"   Attachment leads to jealousy

"   The good sleeps at night while the evil eagerly await sunrise.

03 / "   Now I realize that Sharon took the love, Nita took the Trust

"   Show me a man without conscience and I will show you a man six feet under.

"   Beware of the treacherous friend even when he's apologized.

"   Sometimes in life, try to stoop if you want to conquer

"   The best way to kill a foe is by making him a friend

"   There's nothing worse than unrequited love

"   Love is like two edged sword, it can attack or defend you.

"   Do me a favour, don't fall in love. (?)

04 / "   Most times it takes 2 to play the game, just try to be winning 1

05 / "   Only the guilty fear judgment in a just society.

"   If you care for something, don't restrain it, set it free and if it loves you, it will come back to you

06 / "   Jealousy doesn't kill, it destroys.

07 / "   Excess ambition leads to greed.

08 / "   The only thing you post-pone in life is death. (?)

13 / "   Its better you create your own goal than to try and surpass another's

15 / "   Some friends, I think I can do without.

17 / "   Erasing the memory of a loved one is a tough task.

23 / "   I realize that waiting is among my worst hobby.

"   The past is but the beginning of a beginning.

25 / "   One day, there will be a door like the others you've seen but when you open it, you will see the solutions to all your problems.

"   You don't need to make the world peaceful, just learn not to disturb things

"   Without evil, you will never recognize good.

26 / "   Making others happy can make you happy too.

01/05/07   Why is it so hard for some people to express their emotion?

02 / "   It's normally sad to leave, but it's better to leave on high note.

03 / "   What if the wrong one loves you right?

"   Stamp your feet and be firm about it, the man will show

05 / "   What you see may not be what it seems

"   Justice and law are two separate issues.

06 / "   Can someone be beyond redemption?

08 / "   Walk away from gloom fast before it overshadows you.

"   Being busy drives away gloom.

"   In the battle of love, don't be the looser, it will be disastrous to your soul.

09 / "   Do to others, what you want them to do to you.

"   Before acting, consider your action receiver.

"   Alcohol dims the conscious and illuminate the unconscious

10 / "   Keep your emotion on the leash before it leads you to undesired situation.

"   Sometimes, it will be good if you don't seek the truth, just let the matter lay.

"   They are thing that will happen and you pretend it never happened.

"   Nothing is eternal but eternity.

"   Don't take it too serious because all things will come to an end

"   Easy come, easy gone.

11 / "   Don't let anybody tell you, you cant do anything.

"   Create your dream and protect it.

13 / "   Sometimes in life, you make an enemy without knowing.

16 / "   Did you make your name or did your name make you?

18 / "   Don't mistake my gentility for stupidity.

19 / "   Training is nothing, will is everything.

" Your anger gives you great power but if you don't control it, it will destroy you.

" Justice is about harmony, while revenge is about satisfaction.

22 / " Don't let fear run your life.

23 / " The distance between insanity and genius us measured by success.

27 / " If love's so nice, tell why it hurts so much?

03/06/07 How do you afflict pain to someone without feeling?

" Before you cross the road, check you left and right.

09 / " Don't pretend what you don feel. It irks me.

13 / " I've discovered that I prefer anger to sadness.

22 / " In this our society, the hero is the one who live to tell the story

" He, who fights with caution, lives to fight another day.

02/07/07 "Not a Man", do I rise up to the challenge or retreat?

03 / " Amara, am confused, you are jealous for me, does it mean you care? Because you never show care.

08 / " The best way to fool the wise man is by being his fool.

10 / " Are you truly in love or in love with the idea of being in love.

18 / " Some goes and never return because there's no one to welcome them.

23 / " In every problem, try and see the brighter side. I've done it and it helps.

" One thing I hate more is pretense.

25 / "   The thought of God is not same with man.

"   In some cases, clothes don't impress, they attract.

"   Do you know that surprise is a good weapon?

"   Hide your advantage till you need them.

26 / "   There's no greater lesson than one self learnt.

30 / "   I still repeat, 'mind those you call friends!'

31 / "   In today's society, people don't dress because it suits, rather because it's envogue.

"   Don't you think that some snobbery case emanated from shyness?

02/08/07   They that will win are those that fight with their head and not their heart.

04 / "   Am sorry lady, I have to break up because am coming too close for my comfort.

"   Most men becomes what they dream of, cream well.

05 / "   Don't ever leave a friend that needs your help even if he rejects it.

10 / "   Teach yourself how to navigate in and around the murky water of love, it will help you.

"   Can you comfort someone you don't have feeling for?

11 / "   When two are closely bonded, if one dies, the other dies too. That's why attachment is so dangerous.

15 / "   Rejection! What hurts more?

18 / "   Sometime sin life, you may have to drop some projects even if it hurts to do so.

19 / "   Keep the past behind, move on.

"   Lose grip of any hopeless situation for it drives you

crazy.

" Don't make a promise you can't keep.

" Breaking up is never easy I know, but sometimes you just have to go.

" Rejection, I fear it a lot.

05/09/07 For the fear of being lonely, don't give up on the person you are with.

07 / " Some friends are meant for some particular occasion

15 / " Why don't you think about what you have instead of what you don't have?

20 / " You are never too young to die.

22 / " Don't try to hurt another... because you will inavertedly hurt yourself.

" As you are teaching others to stab from behind. Know that it means you will be watching your behind.

04/10/07 You can stop the clock and not the time.

06 / " Without feeling, your breath is just like clock ticking.

07 / " I don't know who you are but I know what you are.

08 / " Anger is more useful than despair.

" Something's happens sometimes which you cannot change, don't blame yourself.

21 / " In the beginning, it may seem like you are losing, just keep your head up.

04/11/07 There's a difference between the clown and the fool.

"   The clown plays a fool, while the fool is a fool.

17 / "   The longest lasting wound a man can be afflicted with is emotional…

19 / "   I'm beginning to think that I'm not liked, just loved.

27 / "   The difference between the clown and the fool is that a clown is a voluntary fool while the fool is an involuntary clown.

11/12/07   It does not do to dwell on dreams and forget to live.

20/12/07   I think it's losing it's pain (disappointment)

25 / "   The future belongs to those that prepares for it today.

29 / "   The drunk is the one who allows the alcohol to take the lead.

GOODBYE 20-07 WELCOME 20-08

08 / "   Love, can we deny it when it comes visiting?

05/02/08   Bear in mind that the farther your birthday, the nearer your grave.

22 / "   If you can't let the past pass, you might pass out with the past.

23 / "   The past is a guide on how to manage the future.

01/03/08   Every living creature has a destiny. Can you change yours?

29 / "   Which is more bearable, when I'm jilted or when I jilt?

16 / "   I've come to realize that a jilted woman hates and an ignored woman hate more.

20 / "   You can't hide from your past believe me, I've tried and each time, I die a little.

                Clear your conscience, don't side the person, side the

10/07/08   truth.

18 / "   Whosoever that looks towards the sun does not see his shadow.

01/08/08   Great people are ordinary people with extraordinary amount of determination.

05 / "   Sometimes, retreating is more noble than attacking.

08/08/08   It's so funny to note that on an important day, speech eludes you.

13 / "	Winning doesn't always mean being first, it means doing better than you've done before.
17 / "	The more you care, the more you are going to lose.
31 / "	Friendship is often deeper and more enduring than love.
"	Grieve now and save you anger for when you are stronger.
"	Nothing captures a man's desire more than an unobtainable woman.
06/09/08	There's no dishonour in avoiding confrontation.
07 / "	You can't lose what you never had.
14 / "	Men reject their prophets and slay them, while they accept their martyrs and honour them.
20 / "	Decision is better made when there are no options
23 / "	It doesn't matter who you were, all that matter is who you are.
05/11/08	If you can't find a way through the area of attack, then you create a safe zone within the area of attack.
07 / "	Be sensible; know when to bend so as not to break.
09 / 11	I know who she is, but who is he?
18 / "	Death is the inevitable aftermath of life
21 / "	They are thing you remember, and they are things you can't forget.
21/12/08	You aren't free, you will never be free till you have someone love you and learn to love them back.

"   You have to trust and need others to really live.

GOODBYE 20-08 WELCOME 20-09

08/01/09   So often, the things we love the most, we care the least

12 / "   To be an adult and behave like child is indeed a shame

12 / "   I would prefer to be matured child than a childish adult.

13 / "   The best enemy is the dead one.

30 / "   People don't care how much you know till they know how much you care.

06/02/09   Follow your heart when it's calling on you because, because in love there's no holding back.

28 / "   Most times, you have to stoop to understand others.

04/03/09   Do you prefer talking about the past or planning for the future?

"   Time doesn't always heal even though new skin grows over old one.

05 / "   To a pessimist, the glass is half empty while to the optimist, the glass is half full.

13 / "   It is an unlawful act to be law abiding in a lawless society. (Gandhi)

06/04/09   Perhaps I can, but I wont

10 / "   Fear is the path to the dark side. Fear leads to anger, anger leads to hate, and hate leads to suffering.

"   Attachment leads to jealousy which is the shadow of greed.

24 / "   If you get what you want, will you want what you get?

05/05/09   A man's fate is a man's fate and life is but an illusion

03/06/09   I've found out that I give love whereas I don't have love.
    "   I know you can heal but I don't want you to get hurt
    "   When confronted with your worst nightmare, the choice
            is either fight or flight.
30 / "   Love is like air, you never know it's there till you feel it
            and never know it's gone till you need.

02/07/09   A good way to survive an enemy is by total elimination.

??/08/09   Being in love is like a blissful dream which you won't
            like to wake up from.

??/09/09   Wake up from that dream called love and face reality
    "   When love fails, it feels like all is gone.

31/10/09   When the relationship ends, make sure you aren't the
            guilty one.
18 / "   Under a government that doesn't tolerate the just; the
            true place for the good is the prison.
    "   Law does not touch some men, only justice does.

GOODBYE 20-09 WELCOME 20-10

01/01/10	If you can't win her love, at least gain her respect
16 / "	Broken heart men in time, but what's the duration?

17/04/10   Dreams are fantasies that have substance but not material, while illusions are walls built to escape from reality. Yet both are manifestation of dreams.

08/05/10   Have you ever felled in love with someone's flaw?

"   There's always some madness in love, but there's always a reason for the madness.

21 / "   Be wary, some girls come for marriage and not for relationship as you think.

22 / "   My mind has started numbing once more, how do I tell her I don't care anymore?

29 / "   There's no worse death than the end of hope.

30 / "   The messenger is the one who usually get shot first.

"   People try to tell us what we are meant to be , but it's up to us to decide whether or not the label fits.

"   Sometimes things happen that makes no sense. You got to have faith they happen for a reason.

"   To morrow is a clean slate you have a chance of correcting your mistakes and becoming a better person.

06/06/10   You don't judge character from one experience.

09 / "   Supernatural aren't impossible, it's just that we haven't uncovered its secret yet.

02/08/10   It's not our ability that shows us who we truly are but our choices

07 / "   Fear of a name only increases fear of the things itself.

10 / "   The more you care, the more you are going to lose.

"   Nothing's wrong except nothing's wrong.

27 / "   Even a coward confronts the brave when the battle is taken to his home.

31 / "   A friend is just an enemy who hasn't attacked yet. (?)

02/09/10   It's not easy if the road is your driver.

04 / "   Don't compare the present to the past. If you do, you won't get to the future.

06 / "   There's no fun in bending people over if they've already bent.

09 / "   One often meets his destiny in same route he takes to avoid it.

10 / "   Why is it that any time I want to settle down, she turns out bad?

"   Yesterday is history, tomorrow is mystery, and today is a gift, that's why it's called the present.

22/10/10   They are many parts to redemption and not all are smooth

30 / "   Don't judge character from appearance

"   The unsuccessful are the more envious and bitter ones

31 / "   Accident is something that comes upon you and the witness as a surprise (Law)

"   Everyone has the tendency to be angry, but provocation is needed for it to manifest.

"   Whatever thing you have and don't appreciate will depreciate. (E. Adeboye)

"   People don't get better, they get smarter. (Stephen King)